OFF WE GO!
TO MUMBAI, TO MUMBAI

TALKING CUB
Speaking Tiger Publishing Pvt. Ltd
4381/4 Ansari Road, Daryaganj, New Delhi – 110002, India

Published in Talking Cub, an imprint of Speaking Tiger, in association with INTACH in hardback in 2019

Text and illustrations copyright © INTACH 2019

ISBN: 978-93-88874-47-2
eISBN: 978-93-88874-51-9

10 9 8 7 6 5 4 3 2 1

Designed by Aniruddha Mukherjee for Syllables27, a specialised children's content outfit run by the authors to produce books for children on a turn-key basis for various publishers and organisations.
Printed at EIH Limited – Unit Printing Press, IMT Manesar, Gurugram (Haryana).

talking CUB

INTACH

OFF WE GO!
TO MUMBAI, TO MUMBAI

Written by Arthy Muthanna Singh &
Mamta Nainy
Illustrated by Zainab Tambawalla

Hello! My name is Raju and I live in Dharavi.

Yesterday was my first day in Standard 4. Miss Pinto asked if any of us had visited Elephanta caves. We all said no. Then she asked if any of us had been to Horniman Gardens? No.

'I have been to Gateway, Miss,' said Rohini.

'I have also been to Gateway, Miss,' shouted Ranga.

'Good!' said Miss Pinto.

'I have been to Marine Drive,' I said.

'I have been to Hanging Gardens, Miss,' added Saroja.

'Very good!' smiled Miss Pinto.

'But you must know your city better,' said Miss Pinto. 'There are so many wonderful things to see and do here. I am going to give you a project for the whole term. Here is a list of places that you can visit and things that you can do. Try and visit as many places as you can. Ask your parents or older brothers or sisters to take you.'

I knew who I was going to ask. Raghu Dada, of course! He is a first-class guide and knows every corner of not just our Dharavi, but the whole of Mumbai.

'What is so special about Mumbai?' I asked Raghu Dada that night.

'Everything!' said Raghu Dada. 'It is *jhakaas*! Some people call it Mumbai. Some people call it Bombay. Actually, it was called Mumbai first. Then it was changed to Bombay. And now it is back to Mumbai! It is a loooooooong story!'

'What story?' I asked

BOMBAY AS DOWRY!
When Catherine de Braganza, a princess from Portugal, married King Charles II of England, the main island of Bombay came to the British as part of dowry! Can you imagine that?

AAMCHI MUMBAI!

BOM BAHIA !

We shall call it BOMBAY !

'Many, many years ago, the local Koli fishermen and women who prayed to Goddess Mumbadevi called the place where they lived Mumbai,' Dada replied.

'The Portuguese came from Portugal and they called the place Bom Bahia. It sounds like Bombay, doesn't it?'

I nodded.

'Then the British changed the city's name to Bombay. In 1995, it was changed back to Mumbai!'

'When would it become Bombay again?' I asked.

Dada smiled and shrugged his shoulders.

'Do you know that Mumbai used to be seven separate islands?' he asked me.

'Seven? Can't be!' I said.

'Don't believe me? Start counting:

1. Isle of Bombay
2. Colaba
3. Old Woman's Island
4. Mahim
5. Mazgaon
6. Parel
7. Worli.'

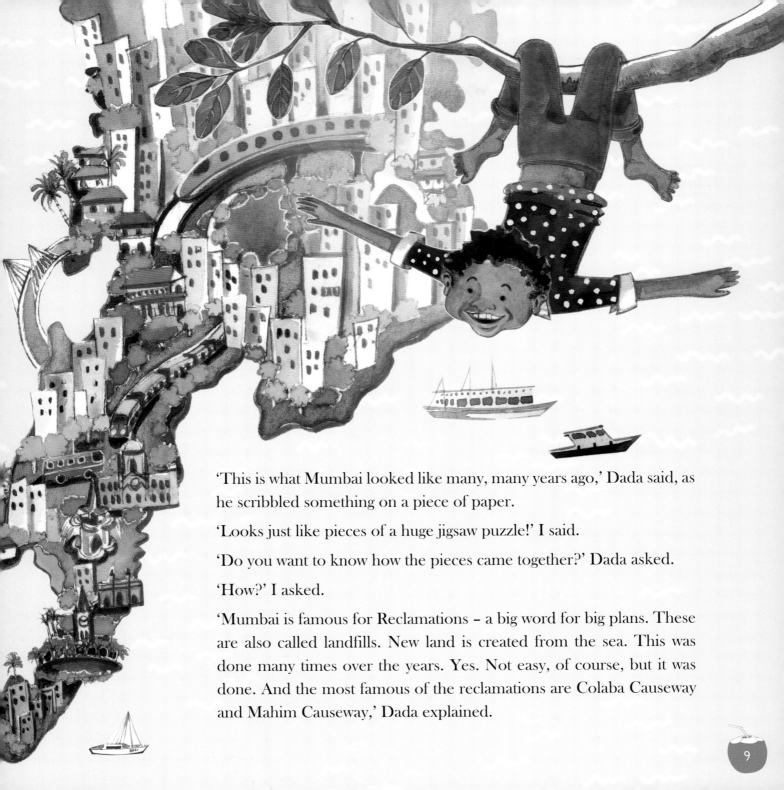

'This is what Mumbai looked like many, many years ago,' Dada said, as he scribbled something on a piece of paper.

'Looks just like pieces of a huge jigsaw puzzle!' I said.

'Do you want to know how the pieces came together?' Dada asked.

'How?' I asked.

'Mumbai is famous for Reclamations – a big word for big plans. These are also called landfills. New land is created from the sea. This was done many times over the years. Yes. Not easy, of course, but it was done. And the most famous of the reclamations are Colaba Causeway and Mahim Causeway,' Dada explained.

'I know Mahim Causeway!' I exclaimed. 'My friend Ganesh lives in Machhimar Nagar of the Koliwada area there! Last year he invited me for the Narali Poornima festival. How we danced! What yummy food – the tastiest *macchi* I ever had.'

'Now you know how the place got its name, don't you? Ah-ha!' said Dada.

'And there were so many fishing boats too. Must have been more than 200. They were so, so colourful! The Kolis really love the sea. So do I! The sea breeze, the waves splashing on the beach, some fried masala fish on my plate...*jhakaas*! You should see the fish market in front of Ganesh's Koliwada. So many fish! So much noise! I want to go fishing with Ganesh's father one day.'

'For now, go to sleep,' Raghu Dada said, ruffling my hair.

FIRST IN MUMBAI

Did you know that the Kolis were the very first people of Mumbai? They were here much before the English, much before the Portuguese, much before everybody.

When Raghu Dada told me on Saturday that he was going to start my Mumbai Darshan by taking me to the Kanheri Caves in the middle of Sanjay Gandhi National Park, I was so excited. I thought I was going to see the wild animals also. We took a local to Borivali station and then a bus. I asked Dada why we couldn't see the animals first, but my Dada is soooo *khadoos*. I love him and all, but sometimes...

I was very surprised to find out when we reached that Kanheri Caves are a group of 109 very, very old caves. I liked the Chaitya cave the best. What a huge statue of Buddha there was! Raghu Dada said that these caves used to be Buddhist Viharas used for studying, meditating and even sleeping. I tried to lie down on the stone bed. It was very hard. Very old.

'It is too late to see the animals now,' Dada said. 'Some other time, very soon, I promise.'

There are more than fourteen forts in Mumbai. Have you seen any of them? Raghu Dada has.

On Sunday, Dada showed me the Riwa Fort, also known as Kala Qilla (Black Fort), on the banks of the Mithi River right here in Dharavi. The castle was used as a watchtower, when the Portuguese were here many, many years ago.

Next on our list are Madh Fort (Versova Fort) and Dongri Fort. I hope Dada takes me there soon.

I told you I love the sea, right? So when Raghu Dada told me that he was taking me to Elephanta Caves next Saturday, all I could think of was the boat-ride. We took the local to CSMT. By the way, the name of this station has been changed four times! From Bori Bunder to Victoria Terminus (VT) to Chhatrapati Shivaji Terminus (CST) to Chhatrapati Shivaji Maharaj Terminus (CSMT)! We took a bus from there to Gateway. For many years I did not know that VT was the short form for Victoria Terminus. Do you know who Victoria was? She was the Queen of England.

All the ticket-sellers for the ferry were shouting 'ELEPHANTAAA...ELEPHANTAAA!' loudly. We sat on the top deck. *Mazaa aaya*! In one hour we reached Elephanta Island in the middle of Mumbai Harbour. We walked from the jetty to the caves. There were seven temple caves there. Beautiful! I've seen so many caves in *amchi* Mumbai. Do you have caves in your city or town?

15

We came back early from Elephanta. We did not have to rush home so we spent some time near the Gateway of India. Raghu Dada told me that it was built to celebrate the visit of King George V and Queen Mary of England to Mumbai more than 100 years ago. It took four years to build this 83-feet tall structure.

Dada bought ice cream and peanuts. We walked up and down from Taj Hotel to Radio Club, munching away. We sat on the parapet wall...waves splashing down below...breeze blowing. Good time-pass.

We then took a bus to CSMT.

'Look up, up, up, and you will see first-class carvings,' said Dada. They were beautiful!

We took a local to Sion and walked home from the station.

The dabbawalas in Mumbai are the best! Because of them, so many people who go to office all over the city get hot, hot lunches every day from Monday to Friday. Sonawane Maama who lives behind our house is a dabbawala. He goes by cycle to collect full dabbas in Sion first. Then he goes by local to CSMT with other dabbawalas.

Homes – Sion – CSMT – Nariman Point.

In the afternoon, he brings the empty dabbas back.

The next day Dada said that it would be a good idea to go to South Mumbai by train, walk around and take a local from Churchgate back home.

'Yes!' I shouted.

Can you guess which building has eight columns, thirty steps and is in the Fort area of South Mumbai?

Psst...The Asiatic Society Town Hall! Everyone calls it Asiatic Library. Dada and I went there from CSMT.

It was lunchtime, so we bought *vada pav* from outside the gate of Horniman Circle Gardens, sat under the trees, ate and then just lay on the grass.

CAN YOU BELIEVE THIS?

Chhatrapati Shivaji Maharaj Vastu Sangrahalaya (CSMVS), which is also in Fort, has about 50,000 lovely things to see: sculptures, very small paintings, things from China and Japan. This museum used to be called Prince of Wales Museum.

We then walked to Kala Ghoda, which means Black Horse. Raghu Dada told me that there used to be a statue of King Edward VII on a black horse before. It was removed many years ago and for more than fifty years there was no statue. In 2017 a new statue of a black horse was put in the same place. There is no one on this horse. I wish I could be the rider!

TIME, PLEASE?

Raghu Dada told me that the Rajabhai Clock Tower in the Fort campus of Mumbai University was designed by Sir George Gilbert Scott. Next time you are in the area, try to listen to the tune, which plays out every fifteen minutes from the tower.

'Shall we go home now?' Dada asked.

I suddenly remembered what Saroja had said.

'Can we go to Hanging Gardens, Dada? Please!'

No more walking! We took a red **BEST** bus from Regal to Malabar Hill.

The Hanging Gardens are not hanging at all! I had so much fun! You must climb into the BIG Boot House. Some people call it the 'Old Woman's Shoe'. I don't know why. Raghu Dada does not know either. Do you know why?

We watched the best sunset over the sea from there.

Dada had a plan for next Sunday too.

'Marine Drive is the best road in the world! But only on a Sunday morning when there are very few cars,' he said. 'Let's go there.'

He was right. We could hear the sea and the birds. A few people were walking on Chowpatty Beach. Raghu Dada bought *bhel puri* for me and *sev puri* for himself.

The road is in the shape of a big **C.**

'Do you know why this road is called the Queen's Necklace?' Dada asked. 'At night, if you look down from the top of one of the tall buildings on this road, the street lights look like pearls on a necklace. I will show you one day, I know the chowkidar of Krishna Mahal. See, that building there.'

I like to travel by local trains. Raghu Dada says that more than 6 million people travel by local every day! He is one of them.

BANDRA-WORLI SEALINK/SCLR

The Bandra-Worli Sealink is a long, world-class cable bridge which is a short-cut from Bandra to Worli. Dada said that it now takes just ten minutes to come from Bandra to Worli. It was built to save time and make the Mahim Causeway less crowded. Two-wheelers (*matlab*, bikes and scooters) and pedestrians are not allowed on it. More than 40,000 people travel on this every day! I haven't been on it. Have you?

The Santacruz–Chembur Link Road (SCLR), is a 6.45-kilometre-long, six-lane road, connecting the Western Express Highway in Santacruz with the Eastern Express Highway in Chembur.

The most enjoyable way to go around Mumbai is on a BEST double-decker bus! Dada took
Ganesh, Nikhil and me for a ride one evening on Bus Number 138 from Backbay Depot.

We sat in the front seats on the top, munching guavas and singing – *Bombay se aaya mera dost*...loudly. Dada sat down below. When we reached Machhimar Nagar in Colaba, Ganesh got off.

Hey, take a ride quickly! They are going to stop the double-decker buses soon.

When we got off the bus at CSMT, Dada saw Amma's brother, Naveen Maama! He is a Kaali-Peeli taxi driver. Everyone in Mumbai knows that Kaali-Peeli taxi drivers are honest and very polite. They also like to *gup-shup* a lot. Naveen Maama talks a lot too. He gave us a ride back home.

Amma, Appa, Dada and I went to Haji Ali Dargah on Saturday. It is on a very small island in the Worli Bay. We walked across a thin, long bridge with the sea on both sides. Appa said that many people say that Haji Ali Dargah is looking after Mumbai.

'We should go to the Afghan Church in Navy Nagar someday, Raju,' Amma said. 'It was built by the British in memory of the soldiers who had died in the First Afghan War. The stained glass windows are so beautiful.'

'We can also take you to the Knesset Eliyahoo synagogue in Colaba, where the Jews pray,' Appa said. 'It is beautiful inside.'

My family and I visited the Mahalaxmi temple the next Saturday. It is right next to the sea.

'Next week,' said Raghu Dada, 'Siddhivinayak Ganapati Mandir in Prabhadevi. Good idea?'

I nodded.

Miss Pinto's friend, Freny Aunty, invited my class to her house in Dadar Parsi Colony last week. She made yummy, yummy caramel custard for all of us.

Miss Pinto told us to try and have a pot luck party at our homes. She said a pot luck party means that everyone brings one dish. Amma said I could invite four people on Saturday. Manu brought mint chutney sandwiches, Ganesh brought fish fry, Nikhil brought dum aalu and Sulaiman brought mutton kebabs. Amma made masala dosas and Dada came home with a huge box of pastries from Monginis! What a surprise! We were all so full.

On Sunday, Dada and Amma took me to Colaba Causeway to see my first English film in a movie hall at Regal Cinema. It was called *The Jungle Book*.

I ate so much popcorn!

REGAL FIRST!

The first film that was shown at Regal was a Laurel and Hardy film.

28

At home that evening we all watched a Hindi film *Ra. One* and a Tamil film *Enthiran* on TV. I like Shah Rukh Khan and Rajinikanth. Especially Rajinikanth when he says – 'I say, mind it!'

I love to dance. I can dance better than any hero. Really. Even better than Hrithik Roshan or Prabhu Deva! I practice everyday. Watch me!

At night, I asked Dada why Hindi cinema is called Bollywood. He said that most films in our country are made in the Hindi language, and are made in Mumbai which used to be called Bombay. Hollywood in America is where English cinema is made. So a mixture of Bombay and Hollywood became Bollywood. Simple. Dada knows everything! Hey, how many Bollywood films have you seen?

I have asked Raghu Dada so many times to take me to a film shooting location. He always says no. On Sunday, he came rushing into our home and pulled me out of my chair. I kept asking, 'What?', 'Where?' No reply.

I sat behind him on his cycle and we were off. Through the gullies, on the pavements – zip, zip, zip! I could see all the bright lights before we reached a large field. And then I heard – 'LIGHTS! CAMERA! ACTION!' I was so excited! Look at what I saw?

Nikhil told me in class that there was going to be a Tamasha that evening near his home. What fun it was! Tamasha is a traditional form of Marathi theatre, with singing and dancing. Some Hindi movies have also included Tamasha-themed songs, known as Lavanis. Have you ever watched a Tamasha?

Lavani music is very popular here. It is the kind of music that you just cannot forget.

I love to eat, okay. But Amma complains to everyone that I will eat any amount of snacks on the streets of Mumbai, but when I have to eat a meal, I make a big fuss.

We have the best street food in the world! My favourite Mumbaiyya street food is *bhel puri*.

IDLI 30
SADA DOSA 42
RAVA DOSA 45
ONION RAVA 55
UTTAPPAM 44
ULUNDU DOSA 48
BAJJI 38
MYSORE SADA 48
DAHI VADA 50
DAHI BHATH 42

BOURNVITA 29
COLD DRINKS
SWEET LASSI 40
BUTTERMILK 25
MANGOLA 25
THUMS UP 25

When we were walking on the flyover bridge of Mahalaxmi station one afternoon, Dada stopped me.

'Look down.'

I saw thousands of clothes swaying in the wind, drying in the sun!

'That is the famous Mahalaxmi Dhobi Ghat, the largest open-air laundry,' Raghu Dada said. 'About 7,000 dhobis wash clothes here every morning. They collect dirty clothes from all over Mumbai.'

We saw thirty-one clean purple shirts hanging next to each other – I counted!

JUST IMAGINE!
Dhobi Ghat got a Guinness Book of World Records entry for 'most people hand-washing clothes at a single location.' *Wah, re wah!*

Dharavi is where I live with Appa, Amma and Raghu Dada. Amma and Appa moved here from Nagercoil in Tamil Nadu nineteen years ago just after Raghu Dada was born. My Dharavi is very big.

Appa is the best sculptor in the world. See: diyas, statues of Gods, mugs, bowls, pots...

Amma goes by cycle to Matunga to teach Tamil in a school. Raghu Dada works as a tour guide.

RAP IT UP!

We have a rap singer living in our gully. Her stage name is Stylish Street Maami, which is funny because Maami also means someone very old-fashioned and traditional in Tamil, and Mallika is not! She is very popular.

I had been to Sanjay Gandhi National Park (SGNP) only once. I wish I could go every Sunday. I love animals.

When Dada and I went on Monday, we saw a leopard run across the road. It moved so fast! Dada said leopards usually come out of the forest at night. I was so scared.

'I saw a leopard! I saw a leopard! I saw a leopard!' I kept saying.

What would my classmates say? What would Miss Pinto say?

DID YOU KNOW?

Olive Ridley Turtles came again to Versova beach to nest! Some people say that they came after twenty years. I was there with Ganesh and Raghu Dada in March when they came. I counted eighty of them. So cute they looked! Raghu Dada said the turtles came back only because the beach was cleaned up.

'The pot filled with *dahi* (yogurt) is hung up so high! How will the boys reach it?' I asked Appa.

'*Ala re ala, Govinda ala*!' everyone shouted, again and again, throwing more and more water on all the boys.

'I hope no one falls,' said Appa.

'Lord Krishna was called Makhan Chor, no Appa?' I asked.

He nodded. I want to take part in the Dahi Handi, but even when I become big, I don't think Amma and Appa will let me.

As we watched, the boy right at the top managed to break the *handi*! Yes! Time for more *mithai*.

The next day in class, when Ms Pinto asked me what I had liked most about Dahi Handi, I said *mithai*.

GANAPATI BAPPA MORIYA!!! I love Ganesh Chaturthi –
Ganeshji's birthday. This year also Appa was part of the
team that made the Ganesh statues in Dharavi.

'I hope our Ganesh statue wins a prize this time,'
I tell Amma.

She nods.

On the last day, when all the statues are taken
through the streets for *visarjan*, Dada, Nikhil and
I danced all the way to Dadar Chowpatty near Shivaji
Park where our statue was put into the sea. (Shivaji Park is
where Sachin Tendulkar practised cricket when he was my age!)

And you know what happened? Our statue won the third prize. See, Appa is dancing too!

I was so happy to tell everyone in class about the prize the next day.

On the last day before the Christmas holidays, we saw Miss Pinto in our classroom with a big Christmas hamper on the table when we went in the afternoon.

'No more classes today!' she said. 'We are going to have a Christmas party! These are special Christmas goodies – nutty chocolates, macaroons with coconut, marzipan candies and Christmas plum cake. You must eat the marzipan candies, they are delicious.'

It was a yummy Christmas party!

Once I came home, I insisted on celebrating Christmas in the house this year. So Amma took me to Crawford Market to buy a Christmas tree the next day. We also bought ornaments to decorate the tree and Santa Claus masks. Dada and I decorated the tree in the evening.

How grand it all looked! Sparkling decorations, jolly Santa Claus, twinkling lights, Christmas parties, carol-singing...and dancing, of course.

At night, we climbed the small hill for the midnight mass at Mount Mary's Basilica.

The next morning, on Christmas Day, as soon as I woke up, I saw a model of a fighter plane near the tree! What a Merry Christmas it was!

VILLAGE IN A CITY

Ranwar Village is the cutest little village in the middle of Bandra. It really looks like a village in one of my story books. And when they have a feast here, no cars are allowed on Veronica Street. We can walk on the lovely lanes around the Ranwar village square area.

I made notes on all my trips, so that I did not forget. After Christmas holidays Miss Pinto asked all of us to talk about all the places we had seen and what we had done.

When we finished talking about *amchi* Mumbai, she said, 'Thank you so much for sharing with all of us. But, there is one thing about Mumbai that all of you have left out.'

'What is that, Miss?' Sarojini asked.

'The Mumbai Monsoon!'

Oh yes! I forgot. We all forgot. In June, July, August and September every year, everything is soooooo wet. Everyone grumbles but my friends and I like to play in the rain sometimes. *Rimjhim...rimjhim...*Amma is always worried that I will get a cold, but I use my umbrella or wear my raincoat. Sometimes I don't. Sometimes the wind turns my umbrella *ulta-pulta*!

One evening at home, Dada played some *dhinchak* music on his mobile phone, Appa made some first-class cutting chai and Amma and I sang. Loudly.

Every monsoon, we visit the beaches, eat some spicy *bhuttas*. Yummy! We are not allowed to go into the sea. It's not safe. Last year once we took a lovely walk in the breeze on Juhu Beach.

Now, let me tell you a secret – I am going to make a scrapbook of my Mumbai Darshan and give it to Miss Pinto. First-class idea, don't you think?

10 things to eat

1. Vada Pav
2. Ragda Pattice
3. Pav Bhaaji
4. Misal Pav
5. Bhel Puri
6. Sev Puri
7. Kanda Poha
8. Akuri
9. Baida Roti
10. Falooda

CITY OF DREAMS

Sixteen languages are spoken in Mumbai. The official language is Marathi. Some of the other languages spoken here are Hindi, Gujarati, Tamil, Kannada, English, Telugu and Konkani.

Dada says dreams come true in Mumbai! I am sure mine will!

10 things to do

1. Become a member of Museum Kids' Club at the Chhatrapati Shivaji Maharaj Vastu Sangrahalaya
2. Go kayakking at Chowpatty
3. Go on a Dharavi Tour
4. Essel World
5. Juhu Beach
6. Imagica Adlabs
7. Bombay Natural History Society (BNHS) Museum
8. Snow World
9. Go on a day trip to Mandwa Beach – ferry from Gateway
10. Take a ride on the open deck bus from CSMVS gate

10 things to see

1. Nehru Planetarium
2. Taraporewala Aquarium
3. Sanjay Gandhi National Park
4. Red Carpet Wax Museum
5. A movie at Regal cinema
6. Byculla Zoo (Jijamata Udyan)
7. Mani Bhavan
8. Gateway of India
9. Colaba Causeway
10. Hanging Gardens

GLOSSARY

Amchi: Our

Arrey wah!: Wow!

Bhuttas: Roasted corn

Chowkidar: Watchman

Dada: Older brother

Darshan: A chance to see

Fatafat: Very quickly

Gup-shup: Gossip

Jhakaas: Perfect

Dhinchak: Peppy

Kaali-Peeli: Black-and-yellow taxi

Khadoos: Stubborn

Macchi: Fish

Matlab: Meaning

Mazaa aaya!: Had fun!

Ulta-pulta: Upside down

About Indian National Trust for Art and Cultural Heritage (INTACH)

INTACH is a nationwide, non-profit membership organization to protect and conserve India's vast natural and cultural heritage. It is today the largest organization in the country dedicated to conservation. Heritage Education and Communication Service (HECS) of INTACH spreads awareness about India's natural, built, cultural, and living heritage. HECS promotes a love for heritage amongst children. It runs a network of heritage clubs. Each heritage club works on promoting the local culture and appreciating the rich diversity of India's heritage.

For further details, log on to: www. intach.org, www.youngintach.org

About Talking Cub

Talking Cub is the children's imprint of Speaking Tiger. Launched in December 2017, the imprint has published over thirty-five books, including those by renowned authors such as Ruskin Bond, Paro Anand, Ranjit Lal, Subhadra Sen Gupta, Deepa Agarwal and others. Some of the country's best fiction and non-fiction writing for children is part of the imprint. The details of all the titles can be seen at www.speakingtigerbooks.com.

GLOSSARY

Amchi: Our

Arrey wah!: Wow!

Bhuttas: Roasted corn

Chowkidar: Watchman

Dada: Older brother

Darshan: A chance to see

Fatafat: Very quickly

Gup-shup: Gossip

Jhakaas: Perfect

Dhinchak: Peppy

Kaali-Peeli: Black-and-yellow taxi

Khadoos: Stubborn

Macchi: Fish

Matlab: Meaning

Mazaa aaya!: Had fun!

Ulta-pulta: Upside down

About Indian National Trust for Art and Cultural Heritage (INTACH)

INTACH is a nationwide, non-profit membership organization to protect and conserve India's vast natural and cultural heritage. It is today the largest organization in the country dedicated to conservation. Heritage Education and Communication Service (HECS) of INTACH spreads awareness about India's natural, built, cultural, and living heritage. HECS promotes a love for heritage amongst children. It runs a network of heritage clubs. Each heritage club works on promoting the local culture and appreciating the rich diversity of India's heritage.

For further details, log on to: www. intach.org, www.youngintach.org

About Talking Cub

Talking Cub is the children's imprint of Speaking Tiger. Launched in December 2017, the imprint has published over thirty-five books, including those by renowned authors such as Ruskin Bond, Paro Anand, Ranjit Lal, Subhadra Sen Gupta, Deepa Agarwal and others. Some of the country's best fiction and non-fiction writing for children is part of the imprint. The details of all the titles can be seen at www.speakingtigerbooks.com.

Arthy Muthanna Singh is a children's writer, freelance journalist, copywriter, editor and cartoonist. She has a diverse range of experience in the publishing industry, a large part of it spent at *Limca Book of Records*. She has authored over thirty-five books for children. She conducts creative writing workshops and dreams of moving to Goa some day.

Mamta Nainy is a children's writer based in New Delhi. She spent some years in advertising before an apple fell on her head while she was sitting under a mango tree, and she had her Eureka moment. She has been writing for children since then. She loves travelling but when she's too lazy to do it, she makes do with reading. She can usually be spotted next to a pile of children's books, chuckling to herself!

Zainab Tambawalla has studied Animation from NID, Ahmedabad. She has worked with Animagic on their award-winning films. Zainab, a mother to two, thinks that there is no better way of capturing the day-to-day fun and craziness that comes with children in the house than doing illustrations. Illustrating for children's books keeps her closest to animation, and to telling stories in images. She also teaches at a graphic design school in Mumbai and is a nature lover.